Tales of Robin

by Geraldine McCaughrean

for Nicole Fowler

Contents

Section 1

Dark Days	2
Little John	7

Section 2

Supper with the Sheriff	12
Queen of the May	17

Section 3

The Silver Arrow	23
A Leafy Bed	28

Edinburgh Gate
Harlow, Essex

Dark Days

Good King Richard is far away in the Holy Land. That is how bad Prince John was able to steal the throne. Now he calls himself 'King John'. He and his friends shake taxes out of the people like pepper out of a pepperpot.

In Nottingham, anyone who does not pay is turned out of doors. Anyone who annoys the rich, powerful barons is put into prison. So every day poor men, scared men, hunted men run away – out into the great, dark forests.

The trees of Sherwood Forest are very, very old. They have seen good kings and bad kings come and go. They have seen robbers and honest men. They see now how these poor runaways suffer. But what can the trees do? In the winter rain they can only weep tears.

Robin of Locksley was no poor worker or shopkeeper. Robin's father had a fine big house and lands. An evil baron wanted that house, those lands. So he killed Robin's father and put the blame on Robin. The wicked Sheriff of Nottingham gladly gave the order: "Arrest Robin of Locksley!"

So today a new outlaw has come to Sherwood. He too has lost everything. He too is running for his life. But Robin of Locksley is too angry to sit down and cry. He puts his lips to his hunting horn and blows.

Frightened faces peep out from behind every tree. Grubby outlaws creep into the open, cold and hungry and scared.

"Come, men of Sherwood!" cries Robin. "The time has come to fight back!"

Robin and his band make camp near the huge old oak tree in the middle of the forest. They soon know every bush and path. They know the perfect hiding places. If soldiers come hunting them, Robin's 'Men of Green' just melt out of sight.

Robin has given them all coats of red for the winter and coats of green for the summer. He has given them bows and daggers, too. He has turned them into a secret army of bandits. They know the very best places to lie in wait …

Oh, beware of Sherwood, now that Robin is king of the forest!

His Men-of-Green rob fat church men and tax collectors. They steal arrows from royal huntsmen. They swoop down on greedy barons and cruel sheriffs. They rob King John's own wagons.

Why, you may ask. What good is gold to an outlaw? He cannot go into town and spend it. No. But Robin does not steal for himself. He has other plans for it.

Last week, Widow May paid her taxes, but she had nothing left for food. Then she found three gold coins under her pillow, and wept with joy.

Poor little Clem wanted to train as a carpenter. But that takes money, and Clem did not have a penny. So think how he felt when he found his toolbox mysteriously full of silver!

At Blind Barty's house, the landlord was shouting, "Pay the rent, Barty, or out you go! Don't tell me your troubles. Pay up!" Then a fistful of gold hit him in the face! The landlord ran to the window, looked out and saw … no one.

Robin of Locksley, you see, takes from the rich and gives to the poor. It is his way of fighting back. He never speaks his full name any more. He never tells his sad story even to his friends. So, little by little, 'Locksley' has got lost among the thorns and twigs of the forest. Now people just call him 'Robin'.

Or Robin Hood.

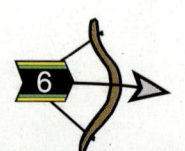

Little John

One day, Robin was walking through the forest, knocking down nettles with a big stick. He came to a river. A dead tree had fallen across it, like a bridge. It was not a very wide tree, but it was the only way across the river. Robin started along it.

He stepped carefully. (He did not want to fall in.) He did not look ahead, or he would have seen the stranger coming the other way. The stranger, too, was stepping carefully, his eyes on the log.

Ooof! They cracked heads and almost fell into the water. The log was too narrow for them to pass. One would have to back up.

Now remember, Robin was a nobleman. He was a leader of men, too. He did not take orders; he gave them:
"Step back, friend."
"I'm in a hurry," said the stranger. "You step back."

"I was here first."

"Says who?"

There was going to be a fight. The birds knew it, the fish knew it. The river knew it, and chuckled with delight.

"Me first, I say!"

"*Me!*"

The man was as big as a barn door — Robin had never seen a man so big. But was he worried? Not a bit. Well, maybe a tiny bit. Was he nervous? Not at all! Well, maybe a little. Did he tremble in his boots? Certainly not! He gripped his stick in two hands and said, "Back up, or I shall knock you in the river!"

"Oh yes? You and who else?" laughed the stranger. He too gripped his stick. "Be a good little boy and get out of my way. There is someone in the forest I have to meet."

"They will have to wait," said Robin and took a swing.

The stranger looked as heavy as a hay cart, but he was light on his feet. CLACK! His stick met Robin's. Then he swung a blow himself.

CRICK CRACK, WHACK CLACK, the noise rang through the forest. Caterpillars and twigs fell into the river, as the men danced forward and back along the log.

Each heavy blow rattled Robin's whole skeleton.

"You fight well!" he panted. "What's your name?"

"John Little," grunted the huge man. "And with a stick in my hands, I can beat any man in Nottingham!"

"Little John, did you say?"

"*John Little!*"

"Well, I shall call you Little John. Ow!"

Robin was a good fighter, but this man was better. He ducked under Robin's stave. He jumped over it. He poked and pushed and pounded until – Uh – oh – aah! – Robin toppled off the log.

SPLASH! He landed in the icy water. His stick floated away. A fish swam between his knees.

"*That* will teach you to get in my way!" said John Little.

The river was cold. Robin's hot temper quickly cooled.

"I need good men like you!" he said.

"What you need is lessons," said the giant on the bridge. "… But you don't fight *too* badly, I suppose. You should ask Robin Hood to let you join his Merry Men. That's what I mean to do."

"Robin Hood?"

"Yes. Haven't you heard of him? He robs the rich and gives to the poor. A real hero!"

Robin waded ashore and pulled off one boot.

"Robin Hood, eh?" he said, and started to laugh.

John Little trotted over the river with dry feet.

"What's so funny? Are you laughing at me? Or Robin Hood? If you are, I'll throw you back in the river!"

"No, no," said Robin hastily. "Just give me your hand and help me up, will you?"

"Give me one good reason!" growled John Little.

"Because I am Robin Hood, that's why!"

The giant with the beard blushed rose red. "I … I … Oops. What have I … John Little at your service, sir!"

"Not any more," said Robin, emptying out the other boot. "Your name doesn't fit you. Welcome to Sherwood – Little John!"

Supper with the Sheriff

One day, Robin was shooting arrows at a tree. (Even the best archer needs to practise.) He was not wearing his green coat – perhaps it was in the wash. So, when the Sheriff of Nottingham rode by, he did not know that this was Robin Hood.

"Hoi! Bowman! I need a good archer! Come and work for me! Be my Master of Hunt!"

"Very good, sir!" said Robin, with a grin. He went, then and there, and ate his supper in the Sheriff's grand house, down in the kitchen.

The Sheriff's cook was not a happy man. He did not like working for the Sheriff. Every time he chopped up a carrot or jabbed a sausage, he said, "I wish that was the Sheriff himself!"

"This is a very *comfortable* place to work," said Robin.

"Huh! I'd rather live in the forest and cook for Robin Hood!" cried the cook. "Now *there* is a great man!"

Robin smiled. "Do it, then! I happen to know that Robin Hood needs a good cook … But don't leave here with empty hands, will you?" Together, they filled a basket with the Sheriff's spoons and meat, his jars and tablecloths and spices.

Next day, the cook left the Sheriff's house to be an outlaw. Robin, though, went hunting with the Sheriff.

Robin led him deep into the forest, crying, "Look! A big red deer!"

"Where? Where?" whined the Sheriff. "I don't see it!" The trees crowded close together. The branches hung low. The other huntsmen were left far behind. "Where are we? Are we lost?"

"Not at all," said Robin. "I know this wood very well, and I know just where we can eat a good supper."

He took the Sheriff to where a fat deer hung roasting over a campfire.

"Are you mad? This is Hood's camp!" hissed the Sheriff. "Look! A stolen deer!"

Suddenly twenty men dropped from the trees. The Sheriff grabbed his reins, kicked his horse, shouted for help. It was useless.

"Welcome to my 'mansion', your honour," said Robin with a low bow. "My name is Hood. You may have heard of me. Do stay for supper, won't you?"

There was nothing the Sheriff could do. He had to sit down on the wet ground, with a pack of outlaws, and eat roast venison.

"Our cook is good, isn't he?" said Robin. "Until today he worked for you."

The Sheriff was very afraid. "They will kill me for sure," he thought. Then he looked at the plate in his lap. "What's this?" he said and held it up. "This is one of mine!"

"Your cook brought them with him. Oh! Your face has gone very red, your honour. Are you sitting too close to the fire?"

"You have stolen my cook and half my kitchen!" the Sheriff spluttered. "You will pay for this, Hood!"

"Ah no," said Robin sadly. "I'm afraid there is a rule here in the greenwood. The visitor pays."

So the Sheriff had to empty out his purse and pay for his supper. He even had to sing. "First they make a fool of me, then they will kill me," he thought. The moon rose like a sharp, shiny knife.

"It is late," said Robin at last. "Time for bed."

Robin pushed the empty purse into the Sheriff's hand. "Good night, your honour. Little John will fetch your horse."
"I can go?" The Sheriff was amazed.

"Of course, your honour. Men who eat together part in peace. That is the rule everywhere, isn't it?"

Robin slapped the horse. It trotted away. The Sheriff looked back over his shoulder, still terrified.

"I will hang you for this!" he shouted.

"Not if I kill you first," Robin shouted back.

The Sheriff whimpered and gave his horse another kick.

Queen of the May

Sherwood Forest was brightly white. It was May, and frothy blossom foamed among the trees. There was singing, too.

Along the path came a lovely girl with pale, golden hair. She wore a crown of flowers. Behind her came a crowd of villagers, all swaying and playing May music. High above, Robin Hood and his men secretly watched from the branches.

"Look! Here is the perfect bush!" said the girl.

A man with an axe began to chop at a little may tree covered in creamy blossom.

Suddenly, Sheriff's men appeared from nowhere. The singing turned to screams. Soldiers grabbed the villagers, saying, "Stop! Thieves!"

"What have we done?" they protested. "Every Spring we come and cut a may tree to carry in the May Day parade! Just one tree!"

"All the trees in this forest belong to the King!" barked the captain of soldiers. "Cut one down and you rob the King! You are all under arrest!"

"Well, I am Queen of the May," said the girl, tossing her golden hair, "and I say the Law of the Forest is more important! Our grandfathers came here on May Day and their grandfathers before them. May Day is as old as the world. Cut, axe man!"

But the man had dropped his axe and fled. The girl bent to pick it up. It was heavy, but she swung it, and a shower of blossom burst round her.

Furious, the captain raised a fist, to knock her down. "You'll pay for that, young Marian!"

Suddenly, a horn blew. Like conkers in autumn, Robin Hood and his men dropped down from their branches. Now it was the soldiers' turn to be afraid. In and out of the trees they fled, chased by the outlaws. May bushes smacked them in the face. For a few minutes, it snowed blossom in Sherwood.

Meanwhile, Robin Hood picked up the axe. With two strokes, he cut down the little may tree. It was too spiky for the girl to carry, so he laid it on his own shoulder. It was dazzling white, but this girl dazzled him more. So beautiful and so brave!

"Now you have your may tree," said Robin, "I suppose you must go home and choose a King-of-the-May to rule beside you."

"Oh, I already did that! I choose you!" Marian's quick fingers had twined a crown of flowers for him to wear. "I have heard so much about the great Robin Hood. Please show me where you live!"

So Robin took her to the Great Holm Oak at the heart of Sherwood Forest. There, King and Queen sat enthroned on two tree stumps, and fifty outlaws waited on them.

"I see men and boys, but where are all the women and girls?" asked Marian.

Fifty faces looked sadly down. Fifty outlaws scuffed their boots in the dirt.

"This is no place for a woman," said Robin gruffly. "In winter we go cold and hungry. In summer, we are hunted like deer. We sleep on the hard ground under sharp stars, and we fight to the death."

"Oh, but I would love that!" cried Marian. "Let me stay! Let me wear Lincoln Green and fight beside you, and rob the rich to help the poor!"

Robin laughed out loud. "I wish! Oh, how I wish …" His hand covered hers. He did not want her to go, but he knew that she must. In the heat from the fire, their flowery crowns wilted. May Day was over.

Robin led Marian back to the path and said goodbye. His heart hurt, as if a spark had burned it. "You will always be welcome to visit us," he whispered. "I shall be watching, in case you come."

"Ah, but next time I'll dress in summer green," said Marian with a grin. "You will need sharp eyes to spot me!"

The Silver Arrow

It seemed as if every archer in Nottinghamshire had come for the competition: everyone who owned a bow. Scores of competitors jostled and pushed, noisy as a flock of turkeys. There was the King's Champion, the Captain of the Guard, several noblemen, a fletcher, a bow maker and at least forty yeomen who knew they could shoot straight. There was even a tired, grubby old man in filthy rags, who needed a crutch to hobble up to the firing line.

"You're too old to see the target!" jeered the King's Champion.

"Too feeble to stretch a bow!" mocked the Captain. But they could not stop the beggar entering. Everyone in the county had been invited to compete for the prize of a solid silver arrow!

A trumpet blew.

"Let the contest begin!" declared the Sheriff, and took his seat. He seemed to be peering closely at each of the competitors.

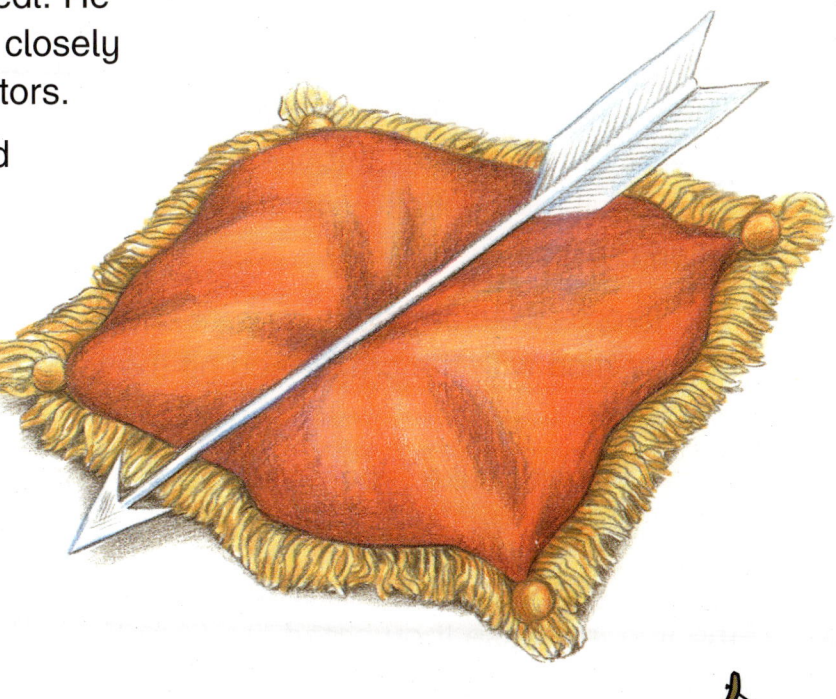

"He hopes Robin Hood will come," said the King's huntsman. "This whole contest is one big trap for Robin Hood."

"Does the Sheriff really think Hood will fall for a trick like that?" bleated the old man. "He would have to be mad."

One hour later, the host of competitors had dwindled to just six. The six took turns to shoot. After each round, the target was moved farther off until it looked no bigger than a football, a tennis ball, an eyeball … It all took so long that the Sheriff had fallen asleep.

The people watching gave a great cheer: that ragged old beggar man with the crutch had hit the target yet again. What an archer!

"Luck. A lucky fluke," mumbled the old man, with a shy smile and a shrug.

No one cheered when the Sheriff's Champion stepped up to the line, because they hated the Sheriff so much.

Even so, it was the Champion who hit the centre of the straw butt. The spectators groaned. No one could beat a shot like that.

"Go home, old man," sneered the Champion and kicked the wooden crutch. "I've won, look."

"I think I'll just take my shot, though," croaked the old man.

How can you improve on a perfect shot? How can you win a contest that has already been won? Impossible! ... unless, perhaps, you happen to be Robin Hood!

Robin drew back his bowstring to his lips and let fly. The Champion's arrow fell from the butt. Robin's arrow had sliced it in two!

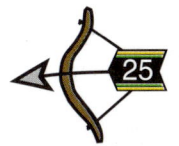

The crowd gasped in amazement, then roared with delight. The Sheriff woke with a start. In front of him stood the triumphant winner, his grubby hand stretched out to take the silver arrow off its scarlet cushion.

"Arrest him! It's Robin Hood!" choked the Sheriff. "If he won, then he must be Robin Hood!" The guard only sniggered at the idea. "He's in disguise, you fools!" Then the Sheriff had to duck, as a crutch flew at his head.

Up on to the Sheriff's horse leapt Robin. The happy crowd parted to let him through. It closed up again to bar the way to the Sheriff's soldiers, but they forced their way through. Shouts and arrows pursued Robin all the way to the edge of the greenwood. (The soldiers dared not follow him inside.) Under his rags, gripped between string-calloused fingers, was the precious silver arrow. Robin threw back his head and crowed with bragging pride.

"What use is it?" asked Friar Tuck, when he saw the arrow. "You can't shoot it, and you can't eat it. Was it worth risking your life?"

"Yes! It was worth it for the look on the Sheriff's fat face!" said Robin delightedly. "For that alone, I would have shot the moon out of the sky!"

A Leafy Bed

Autumn came early that last year. The trees wept red and orange tears across every woodland pathway. Even his own campfire had no power to warm Robin.

Good King Richard had returned. Robin's work was over, though still he chose to live in the greenwood. So many outlaws had been pardoned and had gone home. So many of his enemies were dead and gone. He had seen too much wickedness and done more than his fair share of good. He was very, very weary. When winter cold ambushed him, Robin found he did not have the strength to fight it off.

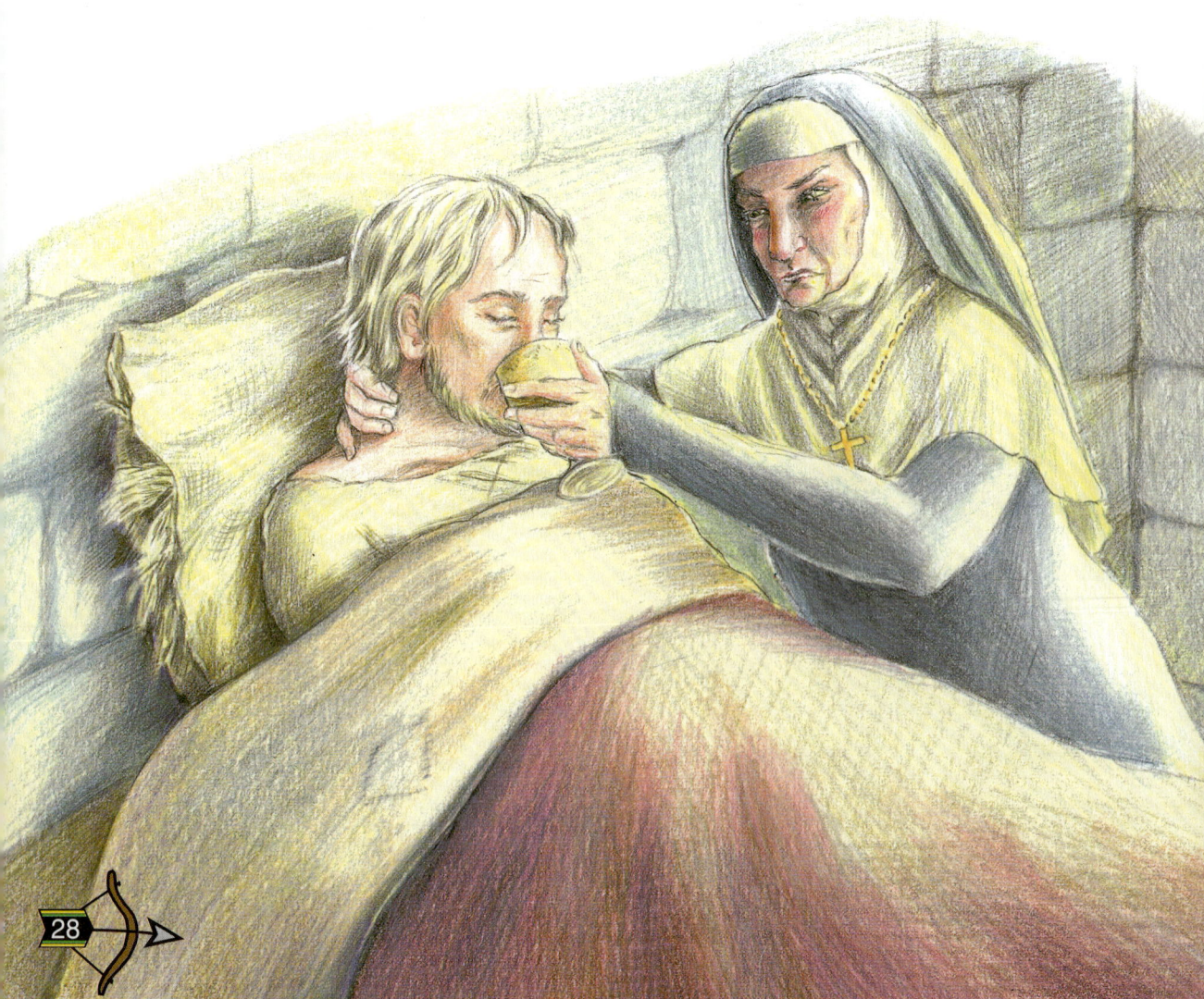

"I must go to the Abbey," he told the last of his outlaws, "or I shan't live to see the Spring."

Will Scarlet and Much the Miller begged him, "No, no! That place is full of shadows. Stay here with us!" But Robin was never good at taking advice.

"What harm can come to me in an Abbey?" he said, and away he went to find medicine and a warm, dry bed.

His arrival set the nuns aflutter like a flock of birds, but the Prioress sent them all away.

"I shall nurse Robin myself," she said. "Make up a bed for him in a quiet corner."

Every day she brought him broth to eat and medicines to swallow. She sponged him with strange-smelling oils. But Robin only felt more ill.

He dreamed that a great crow crouched over him, its black wings spread, its beak gaping. When he opened his eyes, the Prioress was bending over him.

"You are dying, Robin, and good riddance. Do you remember how you fought Red Roger and killed him?"

"I do," said Robin. "It was my best day's work. He was a villain and he deserved to die."

"But he was the only man I ever loved. That is why I have poisoned your food, nursed you with ratsbane, sponged you with venom. Now die, Robin Hood and be forgotten!"

Robin fumbled under his pillow. He drew out his hunting horn and put it to his dry lips. It took all his might to blow one sobbing squawk, but his trusty horn did not fail him. His friends heard it and came. In at the window, up the stairs, across the roof they came creeping, and soon knelt beside their leader's bed.

"Shall we kill the Prioress now, in front of your eyes?" asked Little John.

"No! In all my outlaw days I never hurt a woman and I never shall! Let her crime eat her empty, like a mouse in a sack of grain. Just help me to the window and give me my bow."

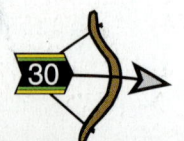

They did as he asked. He drew his longbow (though it was as hard as pulling the bars out of a prison window). "Wherever this arrows falls, bury me," he said. At last the string kissed his lips and he let fly. The arrow plunged into the dense green woodland below, and Robin slumped dead in his friends' arms.

So there he lies, with his arrow for a headstone. I cannot take you there. The weeping trees buried the place under drifts of crisp leaves. Field mice ate away the arrow fletches. The rain rotted the arrow shaft. His grave was lost.

But somehow Robin's name grew larger, not less. His fame outgrew even the Holm Oak at the heart of the forest. Stories of his adventures scurried outwards through all the forests in the land, like so many squirrels.

Now, whenever the wind blows, every ancient tree begins to wag and to brag: "WE SAW HIM! WHEN WE WERE YOUNG, WE SAW ROBIN HOOD!"